D0541971

GLOBAL POSITIONING SYSTEM
Who's Tracking You?

Leon Gray

W
FRANKLIN WATTS
LONDON • SYDNEY

First published in 2015 by Franklin Watts
338 Euston Road
London NW1 3BH

Franklin Watts Australia
Level 17/207 Kent Street
Sydney, NSW 2000

Produced by Calcium

A CIP catalogue record for this book is available from
the British Library.

ISBN 978 1 4451 3870 1

Dewey classification: 910.2'85

Printed in China

Franklin Watts is a division of Hachette Children's Books,
an Hachette UK company
www.hachette.co.uk

Acknowledgements:
The publisher would like to thank the following for permission to
reproduce photographs: Dreamstime: Anhong 9, Martin Brayley 43,
Franant 23, Gunternezhoda 30, Icefields 8, Alex Ishchenko 10, Jgroup
24, Kaczor58 20, Kbkgraphx 29, Leaf 22, Linda Lim 39, Logoboom 31,
Lukaszfus 27, Maggern 36, Mav888 3, 28, Mda 26, Mikephotos 7,
Miroslavtrifonov 17, Monkeybusinessimages 32, Phillipe444 15, Photosky
37, Prestonia 13, Richcareyzim 35, Route66 4, Saorsa 38, Scanrail 33,
Scaramax 12, Shapoval 16, Spanky69 1, 6, Tratong 21, Trish23 34,
Weefanphoto 14; Shutterstock: cover, Balefire 44, Nicholas Belton 41t,
DeshaCAM 25, Featureflash 40, Fisun Ivan 41b, Kaczor58 5, Kamira 19,
Nicholas Moore 42, Boris Rabtsevich 11, Carolina K. Smith, M.D. 18,
Evgeny Vasenev 45.

Contents

Do you ever get the feeling something or someone is watching you? Well, you might be right! Look up to the sky. Every second of every day, Global Positioning System (GPS) satellites in space are looking down on Earth.

Watching you?

GPS was invented in the United States for military use. GPS satellites help soldiers to find their way around, guide missiles to their targets and allow commanders to track troops, tanks and helicopters.

A GPS satellite speeding high above Earth sends precise location information to GPS receivers on the surface of the planet.

FACE FACTS

'On a planet of 6 billion souls, GPS helps us to find ourselves. But it sometimes dazzles us so much that we forget what we still seek.'
Time Magazine, 2009

This driver can navigate the streets of any city in the world by using his car's GPS system.

Using GPS

GPS became common when the US government released the technology for public use in 1983. Today, anyone can find their location anywhere on the planet using a GPS receiver. Receivers are built in to many electronic gadgets, such as mobile phones and laptop computers.

Who is right?

Is GPS improving our lives or invading our privacy? Who should we believe? In this book, we ask the experts for answers to these questions. We will then ask you to become the expert and make up your own mind about whether GPS is a technology that makes our lives better or just a dangerous intrusion.

ask the experts

SOME EXPERTS THINK THAT GPS HAS BECOME SO IMPORTANT THAT WE CANNOT LIVE WITHOUT IT. THEY ARGUE THAT GPS SAVES TIME, MONEY AND PEOPLE'S LIVES. OTHER EXPERTS THINK THAT THERE IS A SINISTER SIDE TO THIS NEW TECHNOLOGY. THEY BELIEVE THAT IT IS BEING USED TO SPY ON PEOPLE WITHOUT THEM EVEN KNOWING IT.

GPS uses satellites in space to track the movement of objects on Earth. Scientists in the United States invented GPS in the 1960s. At that time, the United States and the Soviet Union (now Russia) were enemies. This period was known as the Cold War.

What is GPS?

In 1957, scientists from the Soviet Union launched the world's first satellite, called *Sputnik 1*. The US government was suspicious of this new Soviet technology, and decided to use powerful computers to track *Sputnik 1* as it orbited Earth. Eventually, US scientists realised they could do the same thing in reverse – use satellites to track objects moving on Earth.

FACE FACTS

'The scientific and technological discoveries that have made war so infinitely more terrible for us are part of the same process that has knit us all so much more closely together.' Lester B. Pearson, former Canadian President

Today, GPS is useful in many leisure pursuits. Hikers use handheld GPS units to fix their location as they navigate new territory.

The Cold War

During the 1960s, tension between the United States and the Soviet Union was growing. Both countries were stockpiling nuclear weapons and threatening to use them. It was then that the US government decided to spend $12 billion (£7.1 billion) to develop satellite navigation to launch its weapons. Over many years, the US government developed and improved its satellite system – named the GPS.

" THE DEBATE

The Cold War had both positive and negative effects. Some experts point to the increase in the number of nuclear weapons, which threaten our lives. Others highlight the many advances in science and technology, which now improve our lives. "

Rockets launch GPS satellites into orbit. Here, a Delta II rocket launches a GPS satellite into orbit from Cape Canaveral in Florida.

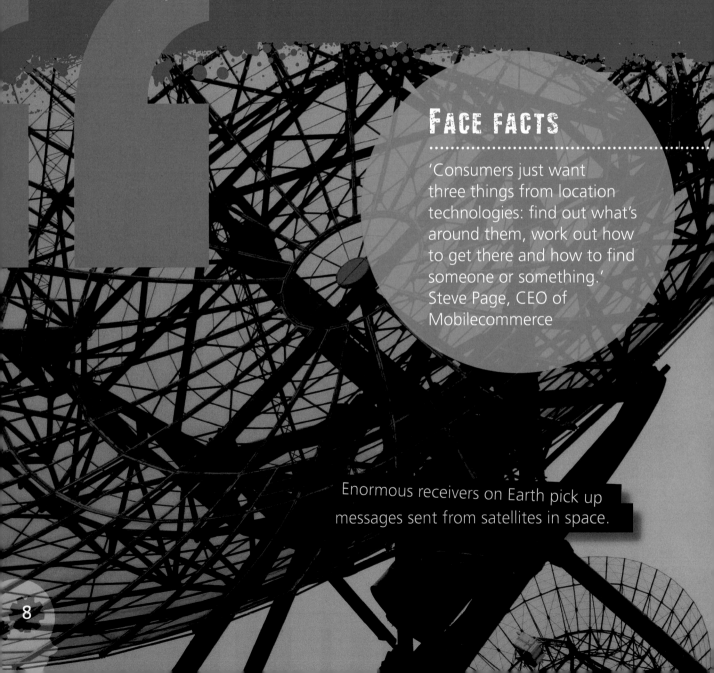

How GPS works

Before GPS navigation, people found their way around using maps, signposts and a compass. Before these pieces of equipment were invented, people used landmarks or navigated their way using stars in the night sky. It is much easier to find your way around in the twenty-first century. A GPS receiver can pinpoint your exact location anywhere on the planet.

Eyes in the sky

The GPS works using a series of 24 satellites that orbit Earth. Each GPS satellite weighs around 1.3 tonnes and is about 5.5 metres long. The satellites are around 19,300 kilometres above the surface of Earth. It takes about 12 hours for a satellite to make one orbit, or one complete journey, around the planet.

Face facts

'Consumers just want three things from location technologies: find out what's around them, work out how to get there and how to find someone or something.'
Steve Page, CEO of Mobilecommerce

Enormous receivers on Earth pick up messages sent from satellites in space.

The GPS signals from satellites are very weak by the time they reach Earth. A GPS antenna on Earth's surface makes the signals stronger.

Satellite signals

Scientists control the orbit of each satellite so that at least four satellites are 'visible' in the sky at any one time. Each satellite sends radio signals down to Earth. The signals give information about the satellite's position. An atomic clock positioned on the satellite shows what time the signal was sent.

Back on Earth

A GPS receiver back on Earth picks up the radio signals from four or more satellites. By calculating the time difference between the signals from each satellite, the GPS receiver can work out your position on Earth.

Most people are unaware of the complex maths a GPS receiver carries out to calculate its position on Earth.

" THE
DEBATE

Companies that make consumer GPS equipment claim that it can pinpoint your location to within a few metres. Many experts argue that these claims are misleading. They point out that bad weather and barriers such as buildings affect GPS accuracy.

"

WHERE AM I?

GPS technology is highly advanced. The system is programmed mathematically to be able to track objects on Earth and then pinpoint their position anywhere on the planet. A GPS receiver works out your location using a calculation called trilateration. The easiest way to try to understand trilateration is to look at the problem on the following page.

CROSSING CIRCLES

Imagine you are lost. Someone tells you that you are 160 kilometres from point A. Now draw a circle around point A with a radius (distance from the centre to the edge) representing 160 kilometres. You are at some point on that circle. A second person tells you that you are 96 kilometres from point B. Draw another circle around point B with a radius representing 96 kilometres. You must be at one of the two points at which the circles cross.

A third person tells you that you are 145 kilometres from point C. Draw a third circle around point C, with a radius representing 145 kilometres. The circle will pass through only one of the points at which the first two circles cross – now you should know exactly where you are!

Trilateration works in exactly the same way in 3D as it does on a flat surface, but instead the circles are spheres.

SATELLITE SUMS

A GPS receiver requires only the location and the distance to each satellite to work out its position on Earth. The receiver feeds this data into its calculations and plots them on a computerised map to tell where you are.

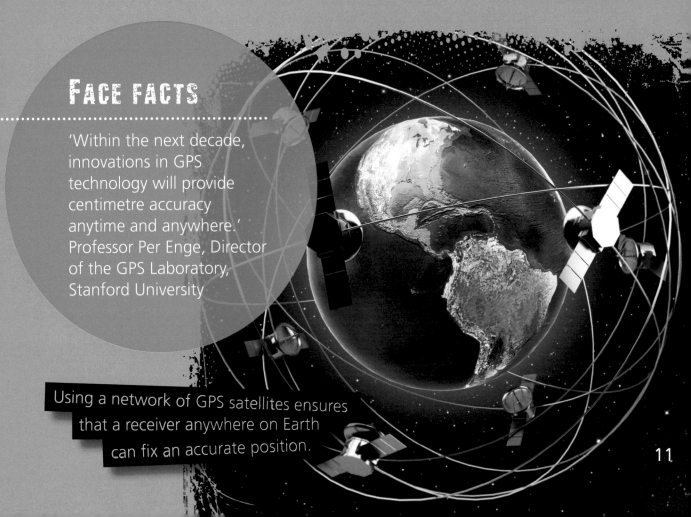

FACE FACTS

'Within the next decade, innovations in GPS technology will provide centimetre accuracy anytime and anywhere.' Professor Per Enge, Director of the GPS Laboratory, Stanford University

Using a network of GPS satellites ensures that a receiver anywhere on Earth can fix an accurate position.

11

GPS started life as a military tool in the 1960s. The use of GPS became common during the Gulf War (1990–91), when forces led by the United States responded to Iraq's invasion of Kuwait in the Middle East.

Military matters

GPS receivers helped soldiers to find their way around the Kuwaiti desert, where there are few landmarks. Soldiers could even navigate during blinding sandstorms and in total darkness. They carried handheld GPS devices, and these were also fixed to military vehicles such as fighter jets. GPS is now vital for most military operations.

" THE DEBATE

Military experts claim that the use of smart weapons has reduced civilian casualties. They point out that satellite-guided missiles can pinpoint an enemy position from thousands of kilometres away. But other experts suggest that smart weapons are still subject to human error. They can still end up killing innocent people if the co-ordinates programmed into them are incorrect. "

In the war in Afghanistan, soldiers used GPS to fix the position of enemy targets.

A GPS receiver and laser system will guide these missiles to their targets.

MISSILE GUIDANCE

Weapons systems use GPS to guide missiles to their targets. Most missiles can now be fitted with GPS receivers, converting them from unguided bombs into 'smart weapons'. The GPS receiver constantly updates the position of the missile in flight, so it stays on target. Unlike ordinary bombs, satellite-guided weapons can be used in all conditions, such as when there is poor visibility, and even at night. However, the use of satellite-guided missiles can lead to mistakes, such as the bombing of the Chinese Embassy in Belgrade in 1999.

FACE FACTS

'In simple terms, one of our planes attacked the wrong target because the bombing instructions were based on an outdated map.'
US Secretary of Defense William Cohen, in response to the accidental bombing of the Chinese Embassy in Belgrade in 1999

BLOCKING SIGNALS

Smart weapons do not always hit their targets. This is because the enemy can block GPS signals in a process called 'jamming'. In this case, smart weapons usually have a backup guidance system to locate targets.

13

EYE ON THE ENEMY

GPS is useful because it can tell you where you are at any time. It can also tell you where other people are. The US military uses GPS to keep an eye on its enemies as well as its own soldiers. This information is available 24 hours a day because there are always at least four GPS satellites overhead at any one time.

ask the experts

Some experts claim that GPS equipment is unsafe because it can target its own soldiers with so-called 'friendly' fire. During the war in Afghanistan in 2001 a surveillance team used a GPS receiver to call in a bomber to attack an enemy position. Unfortunately it reported its own location by mistake. Three soldiers died and more than 20 were injured by the bomb.

Pilots of the US Army's UH-60 Black Hawk helicopter rely on an advanced GPS system to accurately fire missiles.

TRACKING TROOPS

By using GPS systems during the Gulf War, for the very first time commanders could see the position of soldiers and vehicles in real time. This made it easier for them to quickly deploy troops exactly where they were most needed. This gave US and other allied soldiers a huge advantage over the Iraqi troops and was instrumental in the battle to free Kuwait. Ever since the Gulf War conflict, the use of GPS systems has been an essential part of all military operations.

SPYING ON THE ENEMY

GPS tracking can also be used to spy on enemy positions. To do this, some soldiers need to be operating behind enemy lines. They use GPS receivers to report their co-ordinates and those of the enemy back to base. The tracking data can then be used to guide missiles towards the enemy.

FACE FACTS

'Pakistan's armed forces cannot rely on US GPS because of its questionable availability during a conflict that has overtones of nuclear escalation.'
Former Pakistan Air Force pilot Kaiser Tufail, 2014

Soldiers have worked closely with local people to fix enemy positions on the ground using GPS technology.

Soldiers can rescue wounded colleagues by fixing their position using a handheld GPS receiver.

SEARCH AND RESCUE

It is an unfortunate fact of war that some soldiers will be wounded or get lost in action. Almost all soldiers now carry GPS receivers, to show their location at all times. A search and rescue team can use the GPS co-ordinates to reach lost or wounded soldiers quickly. This greatly improves the soldiers' chances of survival.

SURVIVAL SUCCESS

GPS can be used at night and in poor visibility. GPS systems are also useful for search and rescue operations in deserts and oceans, where there are few landmarks. This means the search and rescue team can now search at night, in all weather conditions and in any terrain for lost soldiers.

Aircraft safety

All military aircraft have built-in GPS receivers to reveal their location 24 hours a day. It is important to keep track of aircraft in combat zones, because they are in constant danger of being shot down. GPS tracking greatly reduces the amount of time spent searching for downed aircraft, since there will be a record of its last known location, altitude, speed and the direction in which it was headed.

ask the experts

MILITARY EXPERTS AGREE THAT GPS IS VITAL FOR SEARCH AND RESCUE MISSIONS. THE US AIR FORCE USES A SYSTEM CALLED COMBAT SURVIVOR EVADER LOCATOR (CSEL), WHICH WORKS WITH A GPS RECEIVER AND COMMUNICATIONS RADIO. USING CSEL, SEARCH AND RESCUE TEAMS CAN QUICKLY AND ACCURATELY PINPOINT THE PRECISE LOCATION OF SOLDIERS ON THE BATTLEFIELD.

Army helicopter rescue teams can quickly locate soldiers on the battlefield using GPS, and airlift them to safety.

Public eye

Only the military could use GPS at first. This changed in 1983, when US President Ronald Reagan decided it was time to make GPS technology available to everyone. The decision followed a disaster in which Soviet fighter jets shot down a Korean passenger airline that had strayed into Soviet airspace. All 269 passengers were killed. President Reagan argued that the disaster would never have happened if the crew of the Korean airline had had GPS navigation.

"THE DEBATE"

Some experts believe that the US government has too much control over the GPS. They believe it is keeping parts of the system out of the public eye and using it to spy on other countries. Others argue that the US government has nothing to hide. If it wanted to spy on people, why would it allow the public access to GPS?

One of the US military's most notable GPS success stories was the capture and kill operation against Osama bin Laden in 2011.

Many sections of the media started to use GPS navigation to report on traffic when the US government made the technology widely available in 2000.

WEAKER SIGNALS

When the US government first used GPS, it deliberately made the public signals much weaker than the military signals. This meant the public system was less accurate than the military GPS. Why did the US government do this? Because it was worried that its enemies would use GPS to target missiles against the United States.

MODERN GPS

In 2000, the US government stopped making civilian GPS signals weaker than the military signals. Overnight, GPS navigation became much more accurate for all users. Today, GPS receivers are now found in many everyday devices, ranging from mobile phones to wristwatches. The technology is used in many different jobs, from travel to construction work.

One of the main uses of the GPS outside of the armed forces is for navigation. Ever since the US government made GPS fully available to the public, companies have invented new GPS devices to help people find their way around the planet.

GPS navigation

Today, drivers and aeroplane pilots all over the world rely on GPS for navigation. They are able to reach their destinations more quickly and easily than ever before.

FACE FACTS

'GPS is an essential element in the future of Intelligent Transportation Systems (ITS), encompassing a broad range of communications-based information and electronics technologies and advanced driver assistance systems.'
Robert Crane, Senior US Homeland Security Advisor

Many modern cars are now fitted with GPS units as standard.

Air traffic controllers use GPS navigation to guide aircraft on the runway and during take-off and landing.

Navigating with GPS

GPS units are common in cars and trucks. They help drivers find their way around in unfamiliar places. GPS technology now features computerised maps to show drivers the very best route for their journey.

Using GPS

To use the GPS unit system, the driver enters their destination's postcode or address, and the GPS device guides them there. It tells the driver if he or she has taken a wrong turn. However, there can be problems with the system. Drivers can take the wrong routes if they do not update their systems regularly with information about road closures and other changes.

Air traffic

Aeroplane pilots rely on GPS for navigation, too. It is especially useful when flying over huge oceans with no landmarks, when landing in bad weather and for identifying hazards such as mountains. Pilots can plan routes more efficiently using GPS, and thus save fuel. GPS also allows aircraft to land in remote locations, where there are no ground-based navigation systems to guide them into landing.

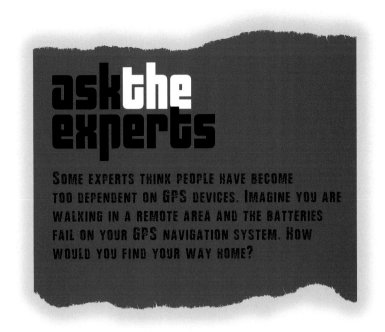

ask the experts

SOME EXPERTS THINK PEOPLE HAVE BECOME TOO DEPENDENT ON GPS DEVICES. IMAGINE YOU ARE WALKING IN A REMOTE AREA AND THE BATTERIES FAIL ON YOUR GPS NAVIGATION SYSTEM. HOW WOULD YOU FIND YOUR WAY HOME?

GPS FOR FUN

Many different sports benefit from GPS technology. GPS receivers are small – some can even be built into wristwatches. Athletes use them in training to record the distance they cover, the time spent exercising and their average speed. If worn during a race, the athlete can download the information onto a computer afterwards. They can then study the data to assess their performance and fitness.

It is now easy to find your way on a long walk using a GPS device.

Finding the way

One of the main dangers for a person during outdoor activities such as mountaineering and hiking is becoming lost. Using GPS devices with built-in electronic maps, people can pinpoint their exact location all the time. Unlike paper maps, electronic maps can be updated regularly, and can be used in poor weather and at night.

Finding the green

Many golfers are using golf GPS systems on their smartphones to improve their performance. A GPS receiver can be used to estimate how far a golfer has to hit the ball, and the distance to the green. This is useful because it helps the golfer to select the correct club for the next shot.

Face facts

'In the future, GPS or other tracking devices will be linked to media coverage, so that fans can view real-time performance data of players during competition.'
Alan Ruddock, Professor of Sports Physiology at Sheffield University

Cyclists wear wristwatches with built-in GPS devices to stay on the right path.

23

GPS IN INDUSTRY

Many industries now also rely on GPS technology. In construction, heavy-duty machines, such as excavators, often come equipped with GPS guidance systems for precision movement. These GPS machines allow operators to move loads into position, often to within centimetres, making them far more accurate than ever before.

The huge parts of this aircraft carrier were put together using GPS-guided machines.

Farmers use GPS-equipped tractors to plant crops more accurately. The GPS units help them steer in a straight line and apply chemicals to crops more successfully.

SITE MAPS

One of the most important parts of using GPS in construction is having an accurate site map. Engineers create an electronic site map and feed it into the GPS system. In this way, an operator can see how deep he or she is digging by comparing the actual location of the machine to the electronic map.

FISHING SUCCESS

Sailors rely on GPS technology for safe and accurate navigation at sea. The ship's captain must know the exact position, speed and heading of the ship to arrive at the correct destination. This is also important when the captain needs to navigate the ship through extremely busy ports and waterways.

GPS AT SEA

GPS technology is used to find prime fishing spots and return to them time and again. Some units combine GPS and sonar technology to create maps of the ocean floor. These charts can reveal features on the seabed, while knowing the depth of the water can also help fishermen to catch many different kinds of fish.

Many experts think that mapmaking is much easier using GPS than it ever was before the technology was available. Before GPS, mapping was a time-consuming process. Maps can now be drawn on the spot using laptop computers, laser rangefinders and GPS receivers.

Surveying and mapping

ask the experts

ARCHAEOLOGISTS FROM THE BRITISH MUSEUM USE GPS TO MAP SITES THEY WANT TO WORK ON. BEFORE THEY START DIGGING, THE ARCHAEOLOGISTS DIVIDE THE SITE INTO A GRID. THIS HELPS THEM TO RECORD THE LOCATIONS OF THE OBJECTS THEY DIG UP. IN THE PAST, ARCHAEOLOGISTS LAID OUT THE GRID USING A COMPASS AND MEASURING TAPE. TODAY, THEY USE GPS.

Pilots conduct coastal surveys using GPS-equipped microlight aircraft.

Surveyors use surveying devices combined with GPS receivers to draw accurate site maps.

FACE FACTS

'The most effective way to achieve a robust and globally consistent continental reference system is through the technology of the Global Positioning System (GPS).' Claude Boucher, former Secretary General, International Association of Geodesy (IAG)

MAPPING THE WORLD

Modern maps are accurate thanks to the precise information provided by GPS. Everything from mountains to motorways can be displayed on electronic maps. GPS is also useful for places with few landmarks, such as oceans and deserts. GPS data is immediate, which means it now takes much less time to map the physical world. Mappers and surveyors carry the GPS systems in backpacks or mount them on vehicles so that they can collect the information quickly.

GEOGRAPHIC INFORMATION SYSTEMS

GPS information is increasingly being used as part of geographic information systems (GIS). These computer programmes piece together information about what and where objects are, and then display the results on computer screens.

THE FINE DETAILS

Unlike traditional paper maps, a GIS displays many layers of information. Each layer represents one type of information, such as all the roads in an area, or all the cities. You can turn layers on and off to focus on only what you want to see. The GPS provides precise location details for all the different parts of the GIS.

This Californian condor has been tagged with a GPS tracking device to monitor its movements.

GPS AND THE ENVIRONMENT

People need to look after our planet. Human activities such as farming and driving are essential, because people need to eat and to travel. But they are also destroying natural habitats such as rainforests, and devastating wild animal populations. Some experts think that GPS technology can help us balance our needs with the need to protect the environment, too.

FACE FACTS

'Until the advent of GPS tracking, it was practically impossible to record elephant movements.'
Dr Newton Kulundu, Minister for Environment, Natural Resources and Wildlife, Kenya

SAVING FUEL, SAVING EARTH

Car drivers use GPS systems to plan the shortest route to their destination. A shorter journey requires less fuel, which costs less money. Shorter car journeys also reduce the impact of pollution on the environment.

SAVING FORESTS

People use GPS to look at the impact of human activities on remote places. Deforestation in the Amazon rainforest can be clearly seen on satellite images. Scientists combine the images with GPS data to provide exact details about the location and extent of the damage. Similarly, firefighters map forest fires using GPS units mounted on helicopters to help plan their fire-fighting efforts.

SAVING WILDLIFE

Scientists are using GPS collars to track endangered animals, such as Asiatic cheetahs in Iran. They can learn a lot about wild animals by their movements, and this helps them to plan conservation activities. Many pet owners are also now using the same GPS tracking systems to track down and locate pets if they are lost.

ask the experts

BIOLOGISTS ARE USING GPS COLLARS TO PROTECT PEOPLE FROM DANGEROUS ANIMALS, AS WELL AS PROTECTING ENDANGERED WILDLIFE FROM PEOPLE. IN INDIA, MORE THAN 20 PEOPLE WERE KILLED BY BLACK BEARS BETWEEN 2006 AND 2010. INDIAN BIOLOGISTS TAGGED MANY WILD BEARS WITH GPS COLLARS. THEY CAN NOW TRACK THE BEARS AND WARN PEOPLE WHEN THEY WANDER TOO CLOSE TO THEIR VILLAGES.

UNITED STATES OF AMERICA

ATLANTIC OCEAN

oil spill

Gulf of Mexico

CUBA

Scientists used GPS-equipped buoys to track a massive oil spill in the Gulf of Mexico in 2010. This helped to plan the clean-up operation.

Caribbean Sea

GPS technology is not just used for navigation. It can also be used to track people or objects. GPS tracking has many benefits, but people are concerned that it is used for the wrong reasons.

GPS tracking

" THE DEBATE

Many people are concerned about fleet tracking. Supporters point out the obvious benefits, such as ensuring services run on time. But others argue that companies are using the technology to spy on their employees to see how hard they are working. "

Some companies use GPS units to check on the delivery of goods. This is called fleet tracking. The GPS device monitors the exact location of delivery vehicles, and sends the information back to a computer at head office. Managers can check on the progress of the delivery, advise customers of delays and even trace stolen goods.

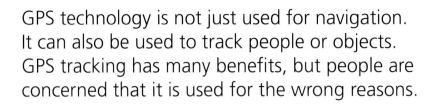

The lorries in this fleet contain GPS tracking devices to enable fast, efficient deliveries.

The GPS units in lorries help drivers to plan the shortest routes and avoid traffic jams.

PUBLIC TRANSPORT

GPS technology can be used to ensure public transport services run smoothly and on time. Computers track the precise location of each vehicle on the network, and then compare it to the published timetable. This information can also be displayed on maps at each stop. The information tells passengers when the next service will arrive.

PHONE TRACKING

Most smartphones are now fitted with GPS receivers. This means they can be turned into live tracking devices. Apple's iPhone has a tracking 'app' that can be activated to find the phone if it is lost. Parents are also using the app to keep an eye on their children when they are not at home. Is this a good or bad idea?

KEEPING TRACK

Parents argue that by tracking their children, they are helping to keep them safe. Other people suggest that parents are using the technology to spy on their children and invade their privacy. Many young people certainly feel this is the case. However, it is likely that this form of tracking will become more common.

31

Using social media websites such as Facebook on your GPS-equipped smartphone means that you can post messages based on your location.

GPS AND MARKETING

More than 50 per cent of mobile phones now include GPS receivers. People are broadcasting their location all the time, whether they like it or not. Marketing companies are using this to advertise products and services to customers based on where they are. For example, they can send discount codes and coupons to people near a shop, to encourage them to shop there.

LOCAL SERVICES

Many customers are driving the use of this technology. Imagine you are out with friends and decide to go for something to eat. You could look up a list of nearby restaurants on your smartphone. The results can then be displayed on mapping software, such as Google Maps, to show you which restaurant is nearest to where you are.

FACE FACTS

'Everyone is jumping on GPS marketing right now. In the US, people have realised there's money in this.'
Pam Kerwin, Head of Strategic Business Development, GeoVector

Social media

Social media companies such as Facebook and Twitter are also using GPS technology. For example, people can use their smartphones to 'check in' to local businesses, such as cinemas and restaurants. Social media websites also offer companies the opportunity to advertise products and services to people who live within a certain area, or who pass by a particular shop.

"THE DEBATE

In Brazil in 2010, a company called Unilever hit the headlines with a high-tech marketing campaign. They put some GPS devices into 50 boxes of washing powder in shops around the country. Teams tracked the boxes back to the homes of the customers, who were given a camcorder as a prize. Many people criticised Unilever for invading the privacy of its customers. However, Unilever argued that it was simply trying something new. "

Most modern smartphones now come with built-in GPS receivers.

GPS games

So many smartphones now come with GPS receivers that people have developed games that make use of the technology. One of the most popular GPS games is called geocaching.

Treasure hunts

Geocaching is a treasure-hunting game that uses GPS technology to hide and locate containers, called geocaches. The idea behind the game is to use handheld GPS units or GPS-equipped smartphones to find your way to a set of co-ordinates, and then find the hidden geocache at that location.

Most geocaches are usually nothing more than a waterproof container with a logbook for people to sign to show they have found it. Larger geocaches may often contain items such as toys, books and other kinds of 'treasure'.

Face facts

'There are well over 1 million geocaches hidden around the world. There are even geocaches in Antarctica.'
www.geocaching.com

Many people are using handheld GPS receivers to locate hidden geocaches.

HIDING PLACES

People have hidden geocaches all over the world. Common spots include local parks, at the side of a street, up trees or even under water. Players use the Internet to then post the new geocaches on websites, so people can find out about hidden geocaches in their local area. They can share photos and stories about them on these sites.

GPS UNDER THE SEA

Underwater GPS for recreational divers is one of the most exciting GPS products of recent years. The device is a waterproof band that is attached to the diver's wrist. The screen displays the diver's exact co-ordinates beneath the ocean, so that he or she can navigate underwater territory more safely than ever before. The GPS device displays a map of the underwater terrain within which the diver is swimming, so that he or she can negotiate any dangerous areas. The device also allows crew back on board the diving vessel to pinpoint the location of the diver.

Divers use GPS devices to locate dive sites in the open ocean.

" THE DEBATE

Some people argue that games such as geocaching are putting young lives at risk. Some players have hidden geocaches on private land, or in dangerous places. Others have put unsuitable items, such as alcohol, in the geocaches. Most geocaching websites have rules to make the game safe and fun for all players. "

One of the most important uses of GPS is in emergency search and rescue operations. GPS saves time by pinpointing the exact location of the person needing help. This can mean the difference between life and death.

Safety first

GPS has become a vital part of the rapid response in road traffic accidents and other emergencies.

ask the experts

In 2011, experts from the Royal Academy of Engineering published a report that highlighted how much we rely on GPS. The experts suggested that GPS is vulnerable to natural events such as solar storms, and even deliberate criminal attacks. They argued that emergency and other services have little or no backup if the GPS system goes down.

Emergency services use GPS to respond to calls as quickly as possible. Emergency vehicles contain GPS units, which broadcast their location back to base. The team closest to the emergency can then respond to the call. This information can also reassure people at the scene, who want to know how long it will be before help arrives.

SAVING LIVES

GPS technology played a vital role in the rescue efforts following natural disasters such as Hurricane Katrina in 2005 and the earthquake in Japan in 2011. Emergency services used GPS, satellite images and GIS to map the disaster areas, assess the damage and co-ordinate aid efforts. Rescue workers also used GPS to record the locations of casualties and the sites of damaged buildings, roads and power lines. GPS was vital because many landmarks had been destroyed.

FACE FACTS

'Data from high-precision GPS instruments show that parts of Japan shifted by as much as 13 feet (4 m) as the fault plates lurched due to the earthquake in 2011.' Richard A. Lovett, *National Geographic*

Firefighters may use GPS units and other scanning equipment to survey forest fires from the air. This helps to target 'hotspots' on the ground.

GPS PREDICTION

Scientists are now using GPS to forecast the weather. They are studying the radio signals from GPS satellites to see how they move through Earth's atmosphere. The satellite radio signals slow down when they hit water molecules in the air. The scientists can use this information to work out how much water is in the atmosphere, and this can reveal that a storm is building.

HURRICANE HUNTERS

Weather forecasters now use devices called dropsondes to track hurricanes. During the process, a pilot flies an aeroplane called a Hurricane Hunter into the centre of the storm. The pilot then releases a dropsonde. A GPS receiver inside the device can detect the speed and direction of the storm. This can help forecasters to predict how severe the hurricane is, and where it is heading.

Pilots guide these Hurricane Hunter aircraft into the centre of the storm to deploy GPS-equipped dropsondes.

FACE FACTS

'Hurricanes and other tropical weather features are very challenging to forecast. GPS will lead to major improvements in tropical storm prediction.'
Xue Meng Chen,
University of California

AFRC
WEATHER

WEATHER WATCH

Scientists are also using GPS technology to study natural disasters such as earthquakes. In 2004, scientists set up a network of 500 GPS stations in California, Oregon and Washington, where earthquakes are common. The system works by comparing the position of the GPS stations before and after an event. Scientists can use this information to measure the size and strength of a quake.

TSUNAMI ALERT

In 2010, the scientists at the National Aeronautics and Space Administration (NASA) used GPS data from ocean buoys to predict the size of the huge tsunami that followed an earthquake in Chile. A tsunami is a series of giant waves that occur when an earthquake happens on the ocean floor. The violent forces shake up the ocean and set up a series of waves that then crash onto the shore.

Scientists use GPS-equipped buoys to monitor underwater earthquakes to try to predict tsunamis.

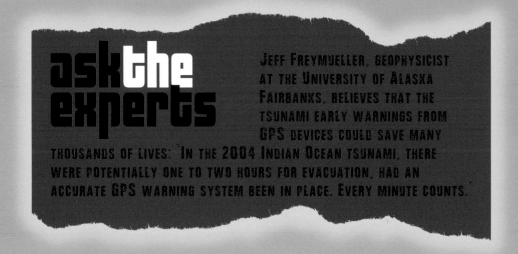

ask the experts

JEFF FREYMUELLER, GEOPHYSICIST AT THE UNIVERSITY OF ALASKA FAIRBANKS, BELIEVES THAT THE TSUNAMI EARLY WARNINGS FROM GPS DEVICES COULD SAVE MANY THOUSANDS OF LIVES: IN THE 2004 INDIAN OCEAN TSUNAMI, THERE WERE POTENTIALLY ONE TO TWO HOURS FOR EVACUATION, HAD AN ACCURATE GPS WARNING SYSTEM BEEN IN PLACE. EVERY MINUTE COUNTS.

GPS has caused controversy in the fight against crime. Police use GPS tracking devices to follow suspects. They can put a GPS tracking device in a suspect's car and follow his or her movements. They believe GPS tracking is essential because it can help build up evidence about a suspect. But some people think it is wrong, because the police could target innocent people instead.

GPS and crime

" THE DEBATE

Electronic tagging has divided opinion among crime experts. Some believe that tagging is a soft option – they think criminals should serve their sentences in prison instead. Others point out that tagging saves money and reduces overcrowding in prisons. Still others suggest that tagging does not achieve anything. Instead, the authorities should educate criminals to stop them from returning to crime. "

Some criminals are forced to wear electronic tags around their ankles in place of a prison sentence.

Electronic tagging

The courts in some countries already use GPS devices to track criminals. Judges can order criminals to wear electronic tags that contain a GPS receiver. The tags are tracked using GPS satellites, and show the precise location of the criminal at all times. The tag ensures that convicted criminals follow the rules of the court, for example, by keeping away from certain places.

Wearing tags

An electronic tag consists of a strong, black strap with a small unit that contains the GPS receiver. It is worn around the criminal's ankle. The system alerts the authorities to be on the lookout for criminals if they try to remove the tag or go somewhere they are not permitted to be.

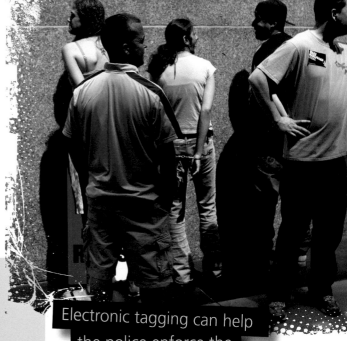

Electronic tagging can help the police enforce the rules of the court.

Face facts

'There is still no evidence that tagging has reduced crime or prevented offenders from committing further offences. What we don't know is what happens to the individuals once the tagging period has stopped.'
Harry Fletcher, National Association of Probation Officers

A criminal is arrested after the GPS unit on his electronic tags reveals he is somewhere he should not be.

Surveillance

Detectives and private investigators are now using GPS to follow suspects. They use GPS systems in their own cars, or secretly attach GPS units to suspects' cars. This information can provide evidence against a person, such as placing them at a crime scene.

Convicting criminals

The GPS feature on smartphones has also been used to solve many crimes. Police use the GPS technology in criminals' mobile phones to track them as they try to escape from crime scenes. In 2006, a man was charged with murder after police used GPS signals to locate his victim's mobile phone in a rubbish bin outside his home. Police often now use GPS to monitor suspects over other more invasive methods.

Face facts

'Recent technological advancements allow for a more sophisticated application of GPS monitoring.'
A spokesperson for Police Scotland

Police officers in control rooms use GPS surveillance to guide officers to a suspect's location.

The police can use the built-in GPS unit in a car to track the movements of a suspect.

WHO IS RIGHT?

Some experts think that GPS surveillance is a vital tool in the fight against crime. They point out that GPS evidence has already been used to convict criminals. Others think that the technology gives the police too much power and that they could use it to spy on people.

GPS JAMMING

Many criminals are now realising that the police are using GPS technology to track their movements. They are using electronic jammers to block the signals from GPS satellites, to stop them from being followed. GPS jammers can be bought on the Internet and cost as little as £90. GPS signals are easy to block because they are not very powerful.

ask the experts

In 2012, the Supreme Court of the United States ruled that the police must get a warrant to track a person, such as a suspected criminal, using a GPS device. The lawyers argued that it is too easy to track people using GPS technology and that it risks invading their privacy.

You have discovered how the Global Positioning System developed from military technology, and how it has recently changed the lives of people around the world. When it was released to the public in 2000, everyone saw the many benefits of GPS. But did anyone think about how GPS could impact our privacy and everyday lives?

You're the expert

Is it fair to use a GPS tracking unit to trace the movements of a suspect before they have even been proven guilty?

FACE FACTS

'The future of GPS will have less to do with technology than it does with politics, with economics and with simple human nature.'
Claire Tristram,
Technology Review

An invasion of privacy?

One of the main concerns people raise regarding GPS is how the technology is being used to spy on people. For example, the police use GPS tracking devices to follow suspects. Parents use GPS-equipped smartphones to track their children. Is it right to follow people like this, just because you think they might be doing something wrong?

A way to save lives?

There is no doubt that GPS has saved many lives in the short time it has been in use. Emergency services use GPS to reach accidents more quickly than ever. This improves the chance that victims will survive. But some people think that we rely on GPS technology too much. GPS may even put lives at risk. GPS systems can distract drivers and cause accidents. Hikers can become lost by blindly following the directions on their GPS devices, and there are no guarantees that the system won't fail altogether. So, has GPS improved or harmed our lives? If you were the expert, what would you decide?

ask the experts

GPS in all its forms, from military use to public surveillance, is here to stay. Experts say that we must develop ways to use the system responsibly to ensure we maintain privacy while still benefitting from its revolutionary technology.

Is using a GPS navigation device to find the way along a mountain pass more dangerous than using a map?

Glossary

app short for 'application', a piece of software found on mobile phones and computers

atomic clock an extremely accurate clock that measures time using the vibrations of atoms

Cold War a period from the 1950s to the 1980s when the United States and the Soviet Union were enemy superpowers

conservation protecting a wild environment and the plants and animals that live in it

deforestation when people fell trees to clear forests for farming or to build homes

dropsonde a device used by weather forecasters to study tropical storms called hurricanes

fleet tracking using GPS satellites to track vehicles such as ships, trains and lorries in real time

geocaching a high-tech game in which players use GPS devices to hide and search for containers called geocaches

geographic information system (GIS) a programme that assembles geographical information in a complex map and displays the results on a computer screen

jamming using electronics to block the signal from GPS satellites

laser rangefinder a device that uses a laser beam to calculate the distance to an object. Laser rangefinders are used in mapping

marketing making sure that people know about you and your product in order to sell more

military all things to do with the armed forces

navigation the process of working out where you are, and planning and following a route to your destination

negotiate to try to work something out, or to work something out with another person

precise exact, without any mistakes

radio signals messages passed through the air in the form of radio waves

satellite a spacecraft sent into orbit around Earth or another planet to collect information or for communication

smartphone a mobile phone that includes high-tech applications such as GPS and an Internet connection

sonar a system that uses sound waves to detect objects under water or measure the water's depth

stockpiling amassing a large collection of something, for example nuclear weapons

tension strain and stress. When there is tension between two people or two countries they cannot easily agree on things

terrain a type of landscape, such as rocky terrain, desert terrain or mountain terrain

trilateration using maths to calculate your position by measuring the distances to known objects

tsunami a series of powerful waves caused by the movement of a large amount of water, usually following an underwater earthquake. Tsunamis cause widespread destruction when they hit the land

BOOKS

Inside Gadgets (Discovery Explore Your World),
Steve Parker, Miles Kelly

Let's Go Geocaching (Boys' Life Series), John
McKinney, Dorling Kindersley

Mapping Earth From Space (Science Missions),
Robert Snedden, Raintree

For more information

WEBSITES

Discover lots of interesting information about the history, development
and use of the Global Positioning System at:
**http://education.nationalgeographic.com/education/
encyclopedia/gps/?ar_a=1**

The award-winning How Stuff Works website explains how GPS
receivers work:
http://electronics.howstuffworks.com/gadgets/travel/gps.htm

Find out about geocaching, a high-tech game in which players use GPS
devices to hide and search for containers called geocaches, at:
www.geocaching.com

Note to parents and teachers
Every effort has been made by the Publisher to ensure that these websites contain
no inappropriate or offensive material. However, because of the nature of the
Internet, it is impossible to guarantee that the contents of these sites will not be
altered. We strongly advise that Internet access is supervised by a responsible adult.

Index